OBJECTIVE TESTS IN THE PRINCIPLES OF ACCO

GW00854549

Derek P. Miller

Lecturer in Business Studies,
Braintree College of Further Education, Essex

HODDER AND STOUGHTON
LONDON   SYDNEY   AUCKLAND   TORONTO

CONTENTS

British Library Cataloguing in Publication Data

Miller, Derek P
    Objective tests in the principles of accounts.
    1. Accounting – Examinations, questions, etc.
    I. Title
    657'.076   HF5661

ISBN 0 340 23442 3

Printed and bound in Great Britain for Hodder and Stoughton
Educational, a division of Hodder and Stoughton Ltd, Mill Road,
Dunton Green, Sevenoaks, Kent, by Cox & Wyman Limited,
London, Fakenham and Reading.

INTRODUCTION

Objective questions can make a useful and effective contribution to the study of the Principles of Accounts, in two distinct, but complementary, ways. First, they provide a convenient means of assessing progress throughout a course. Objective questions facilitate wider sampling of the syllabus than the traditional essay or short-answer question, and thus can more readily pinpoint specific concepts or topics which are causing difficulty. Second, and equally important, they can be used as a positive aid to learning, by promoting discussion not only about which response is correct in each case, but why the other responses, though plausible, are incorrect.

The questions in this book have been designed to serve both these purposes, while providing material that will test understanding, interpretation, technique and manipulative skills, as well as factual knowledge, at an introductory level. The broad scope of the book makes it suitable for students taking GCE 'O' level, RSA Stages I and II Book-keeping and BEC National courses, and for those preparing for the foundation examinations of the professional accountancy bodies.

The first sixteen sections in this book each contain twenty questions and should normally be completed within forty minutes. The topics need not necessarily be covered in the same order, though the later sections do assume some knowledge of basic double-entry book-keeping. The revision test at the end of the book contains thirty questions, many of which require the application of accountancy principles to unfamiliar situations. Throughout, extensive use is made of stimulus material – documents, sets of accounts, etc. – on which questions are based.

Two types of objective questions are used in the book: multiple-choice and multiple-completion. The first, multiple-choice, consists of a question or statement (the *stem*) followed by four possible answers, called *options*. Only one option, the *key*, is strictly correct; the remaining three are *distractors*. For example:

If the sales of a firm are £20 000, cost of sales £10 000 and expenses £4000, the net profit is

    A £4000
    B £6000
    C £10 000
    D £16 000

A quick calculation (which, if necessary, should be worked out on a separate piece of paper) gives the net profit as £6000, so the correct answer in this case is **B**.

The multiple-completion question is slightly more complicated and permits the combination of responses by using a code. For example:

Select your answer by means of the following code:

A if 1, 2 and 3 are correct
B if 1 and 2 are correct
C if only 1 is correct
D if only 3 is correct

Which of the following is/are usually subject to depreciation?

1 Plant and machinery
2 Motor vehicles
3 Freehold land

In this instance both 1 and 2 are correct, so the answer should be recorded as **B**.

It is important that the student should read the stem and all of the options carefully, and not guess at the correct response.

I should like to give special thanks to two of my colleagues at Braintree College of Further Education: Mr P. Allen, Head of Business Studies, for his constructive criticism during the early stages of the book, and Mr J. Jenkins, part-time Lecturer in Accounting, who very kindly checked the answers when the book was completed. I should also like to thank Mrs Sarah Pudney for typing a difficult manuscript; my wife Jane, who checked the manuscript on numerous occasions; and the students of Braintree College for their help in validating the questions.

Derek P. Miller

1. BASIC DOUBLE ENTRY

1 You win a motor car worth £3000 and decide to incorporate it into your business. The entry should be

	Debit	Credit
A	motor vehicles account	drawings account
B	capital account	motor vehicles account
C	motor vehicles account	capital account
D	bank account	capital account

2 A debit balance on Smith's account in your sales ledger means that

A Smith owes you the money
B you owe Smith the money
C Smith has just paid you that amount of money
D Smith has returned that amount of goods to you

3 The payment of a firm's rates from the business bank account should be recorded by

	Debit	Credit
A	bank account	rates account
B	rates account	capital account
C	rates account	drawings account
D	rates account	bank account

4 The purchase of a motor van on credit from Bristol Street Motors, for use in your business, should be recorded by

	Debit	Credit
A	motor expenses account	bank account
B	purchases account	Bristol Street Motors account
C	motor vehicles account	bank account
D	motor vehicles account	Bristol Street Motors account

5 You have returned some goods previously purchased on credit from the suppliers Brown and Co., because they were unsatisfactory. This should be recorded in the ledger by

	Debit	Credit
A	Brown and Co. account	returns outwards account
B	purchases account	Brown and Co. account
C	bank account	returns outwards account
D	Brown and Co. account	returns inwards account

continue overleaf

6   After paying Modern Supplies £100 they inform you that you were entitled to a discount of 2½%. You should

Debit	*Credit*
A discount allowed account	Modern Supplies account
B bank account	discount allowed account
C Modern Supplies account	discount received account
D discount received account	Modern Supplies account

7   The owner of a business withdraws some cash for private purposes. He should

Debit	*Credit*
A capital account	drawings account
B drawings account	capital account
C cash account	drawings account
D drawings account	cash account

8   The owner of a business withdraws some stock for private consumption. He should

Debit	*Credit*
A bank account	stock account
B profit and loss account	drawings account
C capital account	stock account
D drawings account	purchases account

9   A debit balance on the rates account after the yearly transfer to the profit and loss account indicates

A an asset and an accrual
B an asset and a prepayment
C a liability and an accrual
D a liability and a prepayment

10   A credit balance on the rent account after the yearly transfer to the profit and loss account indicates

A an asset and an accrual
B an asset and a prepayment
C a liability and an accrual
D a liability and a prepayment

11 What is the number of entries usually affected by a transaction?

    A One
    B Two
    C Three
    D Four

12 Which one of the following normally has a debit balance?

    A The capital account
    B A creditor's account
    C The motor vehicles account
    D A loan account

13 Which of the following normally has a credit balance?

    A The machinery account
    B The purchases account
    C The stock account
    D The sales account

14 The cashing of a cheque from the business bank account for use as petty cash should be recorded by

	Debit	Credit
A	drawings account	bank account
B	bank account	petty cash account
C	petty cash account	capital account
D	petty cash account	bank account

15 The purchase of a motor car on credit from Ford Sales Ltd. by a garage for resale, should be recorded by

	Debit	Credit
A	purchases account	bank account
B	bank account	purchases account
C	motor vehicles account	Ford Sales Ltd. account
D	purchases account	Ford Sales Ltd. account

16 A cash discount given to a customer should be recorded by

	Debit	Credit
A	customer's account	discount received account
B	customer's account	discount allowed account
C	discount allowed account	customer's account
D	discount received account	customer's account

continue overleaf

17 Select your answer by means of the the following code:

A if 1, 2 and 3 are correct
B if 1 and 2 are correct
C if only 1 is correct
D if only 3 is correct

When your firm receives an invoice, and assuming that when the account is settled full advantage is taken of any discounts offered, which of the following items will be recorded in the double entry accounts?

1 Cash discount
2 Net invoice price
3 Trade discount

18 A cash rent rebate should be recorded by

	Debit	Credit
A	profit and loss account	cash account
B	cash account	rent account
C	rent account	cash account
D	profit and loss account	rent account

19 A building contractor has used his own workmen to redecorate his home. Which of the following adjustments is necessary regarding the wage costs of the job?

	Debit	Credit
A	Drawings account	Wages account
B	Bank account	Wages account
C	Wages account	Drawings account
D	Wages account	Bank account

20 Which one of the following statements is correct?

A A proprietor's capital will remain constant if he only withdraws his Net Profit each year and does not introduce any new capital.
B A proprietor's capital will increase if his drawings are higher than his Net Profit and he does not introduce any new capital.
C A proprietor's capital will decrease if his Net Profit is greater than his drawings and he does not introduce any new capital.
D A proprietor's capital will remain constant if he only withdraws his Net Profit each year, but also introduces new capital.

2. TRADING, PROFIT AND LOSS ACCOUNTS

1 Gross profit equals

    A sales *minus* closing stock
    B purchases *minus* closing stock
    C net profit *minus* expenses
    D sales *minus* cost of goods sold

2 Cost of sales equals

    A sales *minus* purchases
    B purchases *minus* returns out *plus* closing stock
    C (sales *plus* opening stock) *minus* (purchases *plus* closing stock)
    D opening stock *minus* closing stock *plus* purchases *minus* returns out

3 Net profit equals

    A gross profit *minus* expenses
    B sales *minus* cost of sales
    C sales *minus* expenses
    D capital *minus* expenses

4 A man buys £4000 worth of goods and sells $\frac{3}{4}$ of them for £5000. His gross profit is

    A £1000
    B £2000
    C £3000
    D £4000

5 Net profit *plus* expenses equals

    A purchases
    B cost of goods sold
    C capital
    D gross profit

6 If sales are £1000, expenses £200 and net profit is 10% of sales, the gross profit is

    A £300
    B £900
    C £1010
    D £1100

continue overleaf

7 If the gross profit is £500 and the net profit is 25% of the gross profit, the expenses must be

 A £125
 B £375
 C £415
 D £625

8 If sales are £600, gross profit is 20% of sales and net profit is 10% of sales, the expenses are

 A £60
 B £120
 C £240
 D £480

9 An operating statement is similar to a

 A trial balance
 B balance sheet
 C trading, profit and loss account
 D bank reconciliation statement

10 Net sales equals sales *minus*

 A returns outwards
 B cost of goods sold
 C returns inwards
 D carriage on sales

Look at the following account and then answer questions 11 to 16

Trading Account for the year ended 31 December 19—				
	£	£		£
Opening stock		2000	Sales	10 100
Add Purchases	7000		*Less* Sales returns	50
Add Carriage in	100			
	7100			
Less Purchases returns	200	6 900		
		8 900		
Less Closing stock		3 000		
		5 900		
Gross profit		4 150		
		£10 050		£10 050

11 The turnover is

   A £9900
   B £9950
   C £10 050
   D £10 100

12 The gross profit as a percentage of net sales is approximately

   A 10%
   B 20%
   C 30%
   D 40%

13 The net cost of purchases for the year was

   A £6900
   B £7000
   C £7100
   D £7300

14 Returns outwards amounted to

   A £50
   B £100
   C £150
   D £200

15 If the purchases had been undercast by £1000 the gross profit would be

   A £3150
   B £4150
   C £5150
   D £6150

16 The cost of goods sold is

   A £5900
   B £6900
   C £7100
   D £8900

continue overleaf

Look at the following account and then answer questions 17 to 20. Assume that the net sales for the period amounted to £10 050.

Profit and Loss Account for year ended 31 December 19—				
	£	£		£
Rent paid	1000		Gross profit	4150
Rent accrued	200	1200	Discounts	50
Advertising	600			
Advertising prepaid	100	500		
Salaries	1000			
Salaries owing	300	1300		
Rates		200		
Net Profit		1000		
		£4200		£4200

17 The advertising expense for the year is

    A £100
    B £500
    C £600
    D £700

18 The discount entry is

    A discount allowed
    B discount received
    C trade discount
    D prepaid discount

19 Net profit as a percentage of net sales is approximately

    A 5%
    B 10%
    C 15%
    D 20%

20 Expenses for the year total

    A £2900
    B £3000
    C £3100
    D £3200

3. BALANCE SHEETS

1 A balance sheet is a

    A statement of debtors and creditors
    B statement of income and expenditure for the year
    C statement of cash received and paid throughout the year
    D financial statement of a business's wealth on a particular scale

2 Which one of the following is a fixed asset for a builder's merchant?

    A Cash
    B Stock
    C Debtors
    D Typewriter

3 Which one of the following is a garage's current asset?

    A A breakdown van
    B The managing director's private car
    C The Ford Cortina in the saleroom
    D A customer's car in for repair

4 Net current assets are the same as

    A working capital
    B total assets *minus* current liabilities
    C fixed assets *minus* current liabilities
    D capital *minus* current liabilities

5 A proprietor's capital is

    A opening capital *plus* drawings *minus* net profit
    B total assets *minus* external liabilities
    C current assets *minus* working capital
    D opening capital *plus* net profit *plus* creditors

6 Which one of the following is usually a current liability?

    A Mortgage
    B Bank loan
    C Bank overdraft
    D Rent paid in advance

continue overleaf

Look at the following balance sheet after the first year of a sole trader's business, and then answer questions 7 to 16

Balance Sheet as at 31 December 19—					
Liabilities			**Assets**		
					Depreciation
Capital at 1 Jan.		12 000	Fixed Assets	At Cost	to date Net
Net profit		3 000	Land and buildings	10 000	– 10 000
		15 000	Plant and machinery	8 000	4000 4 000
Drawings		1 000	Motor vehicles	4 000	1000 3 000
		14 000		22 000	5000 17 000
Long Term Liability					
Bank loan (15%) from 1 Jan.		5 000	**Current Assets**		
			Stock	3000	
Current Liabilities			Debtors	1000	
Creditors	2000		Rates prepaid	100	
Rent owing for final quarter	100		Cash in hand	250	
Interest owing on bank loan	250		Total current assets		4 350
		2 350			
		£21 350			£21 350

7 The percentage return on the owner's opening capital for the past year was

    A 15%
    B 20%
    C 25%
    D 30%

8 The working capital is

    A £2000
    B £3000
    C £5000
    D £17 000

9 The owner's capital employed in the business at the date of the balance sheet is

   A £12 000
   B £14 000
   C £19 000
   D £21 350

10 The business's external liabilities are

   A £5000
   B £7350
   C £12 000
   D £14 000

11 The interest on the loan paid during the year was

   A £250
   B £500
   C £750
   D £1000

12 The book value of the fixed assets is

   A £5000
   B £17 000
   C £22 000
   D £27 000

13 The net assets figure is

   A £7350
   B £14 000
   C £19 000
   D £21 350

14 The year's rent for the business is

   A £100
   B £200
   C £300
   D £400

15 The percentage return on total assets employed was approximately

   A 5%
   B 14%
   C 20%
   D 25%

continue overleaf

16 Select your answer by means of the following code:

A if 1, 2 and 3 are correct
B if 1 and 2 only are correct
C if only 1 is correct
D if only 3 is correct

The closing stock of £3000 for balance sheet purposes is often valued at

1 selling price for the goods
2 cost price minus ten per cent
3 cost price or market value, whichever is lower

17 In a balance sheet the balance of the fixed assets accounts are usually included at

A cost
B book value
C scrap value
D replacement value

18 Which one of the following would usually be regarded as a current liability?

A A liability due for payment within 12 months
B A liability due for payment within 24 months
C A liability due for payment within 36 months
D A liability due for payment within 48 months

19 Net assets equals

A current assets *minus* current liabilities
B fixed assets *minus* current liabilities
C total assets *minus* current liabilities
D fictitious assets *minus* current liabilities

20 If drawings exceed opening capital plus net profit, and no new capital has been introduced, then the

A business is healthy
B drawings account has a credit balance
C business is bankrupt
D capital account has a credit balance

4. BOOKS OF ORIGINAL ENTRY

1   Which one of the following is NOT a book of original entry?

    A The cash book
    B The journal
    C The ledger
    D The sales day book

2   Day books are used

    A because of the requirements of the law
    B to avoid numerous entries in the general ledger
    C because the double entry system would not work without them
    D because the Institute of Chartered Acccountants state that you must

3   Which one of the following is a book of original entry and is also part of the ledger?

    A The cash book
    B The journal
    C The sales day book
    D The purchase day book

4   The main source of information for the sales day book is obtained from

    A invoices received
    B invoices sent out
    C credit notes sent out
    D the till roll

5   The main source of information for the purchase day book is obtained from

    A invoices received
    B invoices sent out
    C credit notes received
    D debit notes sent out

6   The main source of information for the sales returns day book is obtained from

    A invoices received
    B invoices sent out
    C credit notes sent out
    D debit notes received

continue overleaf

7 The main source of information for the purchase returns day book is obtained from

    A invoices received
    B invoices sent out
    C credit notes received
    D debit notes sent out

8 The totals of the sales day book are transferred to the

    A debit side of the sales account
    B credit side of the sales account
    C debit side of the sales control account
    D journal proper

9 The totals of the purchase returns day book are transferred to the

    A debit side of the returns inwards account
    B debit side of the returns outwards account
    C credit side of the returns inwards account
    D credit side of the returns outwards account

10 Which one of the following is entered in the journal proper?

    A Purchases and returns of stock
    B Sales and returns of stock
    C Cash transactions
    D Opening entries of a new business

11 Which one of the following is entered in the journal proper?

    A Purchase of fixed assets for cash
    B Purchase of fixed assets on credit
    C Purchase of stock on credit
    D Purchase of stock for cash

12 Which one of the following is entered in the journal proper?

    A The sale of an asset for cash
    B The withdrawal of cash for private use
    C Cash discount given to a customer
    D The correction of errors made in the ledger

For questions 13 and 14 select your answers by means of the following code:

A if 1, 2 and 3 are correct
B if 1 and 2 only are correct
C if only 1 is correct
D if only 3 is correct

13 An entry in the journal should include

1 the name of the account to be debited
2 the name of the account to be credited
3 a description of the transaction

14 James Brothers have purchased a filing cabinet for office use, from Office Supplies Ltd, paying immediately by cash. This transaction will be entered in the

1 journal proper
2 purchases day book
3 cash book

15 Best Garages Ltd sold one of their office typewriters on credit to Mills Ltd. The journal entries in the books of Best Garages Ltd should be

	Debit	*Credit*
A	Mills Ltd account	bank account
B	Best Garages Ltd account	Mills Ltd account
C	office machinery account	Mills Ltd account
D	Mills Ltd account	office machinery account

16 Clark owes you £100 but cannot pay cash. He offers you a new office desk in payment, which you accept. The journal entries should be

	Debit	*Credit*
A	cash account	Clark's account
B	Clark's account	office furniture account
C	office furniture account	Clark's account
D	bank account	office furniture account

17 You owe Gould Ltd £24, but receive a letter from Martin and Co. Ltd informing you that they have taken over Gould Ltd and that you now owe them the money. The journal entries in your books should be

	Debit	*Credit*
A	Martin and Co. Ltd account	Gould Ltd account
B	Gould Ltd account	Martin and Co. Ltd account
C	Gould Ltd account	bank account
D	bank account	Gould Ltd account

continue overleaf

18 The position of your business on 1st January is as follows. Motor van £200, Debtors £40, Creditors £20, Bank overdraft £50, Office furniture £100. You decide to open a set of books. The journal entries should be

	Debit		*Credit*	
A	creditors accounts	£20	office furniture account	£1
	bank overdraft account	£50	motor van account	£2
	capital account	£270	debtors accounts	£4
B	office furniture account	£100	creditors accounts	£2
	motor van account	£200	bank account	£5
	debtors accounts	£40	capital account	£2
C	office furniture account	£100	creditors accounts	£2
	motor van account	£200	capital account	£3
	bank account	£50		
	debtors accounts	£40		
D	motor van account	£200	debtors accounts	£4
	bank account	£50	office furniture account	£1
	creditors accounts	£20	capital account	£1

19 Select your answer by means of the following code:

A if 1, 2 and 3 are correct
B if 1 and 2 only are correct
C if only 1 is correct
D if only 3 is correct

Bridge Garages Ltd purchased a new car on credit from Volvo U.K. Ltd, for their showroom. In the books of Bridge Garages Ltd this transaction will be entered in the

1 cash book
2 journal proper
3 purchase day book

20 Bridge Garages Ltd purchased a breakdown truck from Volvo U.K. Ltd, on credit, for use in the business. The journal entries in the books of Bridge Garages Ltd should be

	Debit	*Credit*
A	motor vehicles account	Volvo U.K. Ltd account
B	Volvo U.K. Ltd account	motor vehicles account
C	purchases account	Volvo U.K. Ltd account
D	motor vehicles account	Bridge Garages Ltd account

5. TRIAL BALANCE, SUSPENSE ACCOUNTS AND THE CORRECTION OF ERRORS

1 A trial balance is

    A a balance sheet
    B the balance of the bank account
    C a rough draft of the final accounts
    D a list of the balances in the ledger

2 The main purpose of a trial balance is to

    A help balance the bank account
    B check the accuracy of the books of original entry
    C help check the arithmetical accuracy of the double entry
    D help check the bank account with the bank statement

3 Select your answer by means of the following code:

    A if 1, 2 and 3 are correct
    B if 1 and 2 only are correct
    C if only 1 is correct
    D if only 3 is correct

Which of the following types of error in the ledger will NOT be revealed by a trial balance?

1 An error of omission
2 An error of commission
3 An error of principle

4 Which one of the following errors would normally be revealed by a trial balance?

    A A transaction is completely omitted from the books
    B A sale to Smith Brothers is entered in Smith and Co. Ltd account
    C A purchase of stock for resale has been entered in an asset account
    D The sale of an asset has only been entered on one side of the books

5 A suspense account is opened when the

    A trading account does not balance
    B profit and loss account does not balance
    C trial balance does not balance
    D bank account does not balance

continue overleaf

6 Select your answer by means of the following code:

    A if 1, 2 and 3 are correct
    B if 1 and 2 only are correct
    C if only 1 is correct
    D if only 3 is correct

Which of the following statements about suspense accounts is/are correct?

1 If an error is made but the trial balance is not affected, a suspense account must still be opened.
2 A suspense account is not opened unless the trial balance differs by more than £100.
3 If the final accounts have to be prepared, a debit balance on the suspense account will appear on the assets side of the balance sheet.

The trial balance of Clarkson and Co. fails to agree. The book-keeper places the difference in a suspense account and then discovers the following errors. Indicate in questions 7 to 20 which corrections need to be made. The corrections need not necessarily involve the suspense account.

7 Cash discount to Jones Ltd £10, was entered in the discount allowed account, but omitted from Jones Ltd account

	Debit		*Credit*	
A	suspense account	£10	Jones Ltd account	£1
B	Jones Ltd account	£10	suspense account	£1
C	suspense account	£10	discount allowed account	£1
D	Jones Ltd account	£10	discount allowed account	£1

8 Returns inwards from Powell and Co. were credited to Howell and Co. by mistake, £15

	Debit		*Credit*	
A	suspense account	£15	Powell and Co. account	£1
B	Powell and Co. account	£15	suspense account	£1
C	Howell and Co. account	£15	Powell and Co. account	£1
D	Powell and Co. account	£15	Howell and Co. account	£1

9 Cash discount received from Taylor, £20, was omitted from the discount account

	Debit		*Credit*	
A	Discount received account	£20	Taylor account	£2
B	Taylor account	£20	discount received account	£2
C	discount received account	£20	suspense account	£2
D	suspense account	£20	discount received account	£2

10 Returns outwards of £5 to Jones and Co. Ltd were credited to the returns inwards account by mistake

	Debit		Credit	
A	returns outwards account	£5	returns inwards account	£5
B	returns inwards account	£5	returns outwards account	£5
C	suspense account	£5	returns outwards account	£5
D	returns outwards account	£5	suspense account	£5

11 A cheque received from the Halstead Co. Ltd for £50 for goods supplied to them was entered on the debit side of their account

	Debit		Credit	
A	bank account	£100	Halstead Co. Ltd account	£100
B	Halstead Co. Ltd account	£50	suspense account	£50
C	suspense account	£50	Halstead Co. Ltd account	£50
D	suspense account	£100	Halstead Co. Ltd account	£100

12 The sales day book had been overcast by £65

	Debit		Credit	
A	sales account	£65	suspense account	£65
B	sales account	£130	suspense account	£130
C	suspense account	£65	sales account	£65
D	suspense account	£130	sales account	£130

13 Bank charges of £40 had been entered in the cash book but omitted from the bank charges account

	Debit		Credit	
A	suspense account	£40	bank charges account	£40
B	bank charges account	£40	suspense account	£40
C	suspense account	£80	bank charges account	£80
D	bank charges account	£80	suspense account	£80

14 The purchase of an office desk for £110 was debited by mistake to the purchases account

	Debit		Credit	
A	office furniture account	£110	suspense account	£110
B	purchases account	£110	suspense account	£110
C	suspense account	£110	purchases account	£110
D	office furniture account	£110	purchases account	£110

continue overleaf

15 Returns inwards from Manchester Ltd, £29, was credited to the returns inwards account as £92

	Debit		Credit	
A	returns inwards account	£63	suspense account	£6
B	suspense account	£63	returns inwards account	£6
C	returns inwards account	£121	suspense account	£1
D	suspense account	£121	returns inwards account	£1

16 Cash discount allowed to Thorpewise Ltd, £24, was entered correctly in the personal account but was credited to the discount received account by mistake

	Debit		Credit	
A	discount allowed account	£48	suspense account	£4
B	discount received account	£24	discount allowed account	£2
C	discount allowed account	£24	discount received account	£2
D	discount allowed account *and*	£24	suspense account	£4
	discount received account	£24		

17 A bad debt of £14 which should have been written off J. Carter's account was entered in the bad debts account correctly but was accidentally written off Johnston Brothers account as £41

	Debit		Credit	
A	Johnston Brothers account	£41	J. Carter's account *and*	£1
			suspense account	£2
B	Johnston Brothers account	£41	suspense account *and*	£1
			J. Carter's account	£2
C	suspense account *and*	£27	Johnston Brothers account	£4
	J. Carter's account	£14		
D	suspense account	£55	J. Carter's account *and*	£1
			Johnston Brothers account	£4

18 Returns outwards to Anglia Ltd of £16 were entered in the returns account correctly but were credited to A. N. Gibb by mistake

	Debit		Credit	
A	suspense account	£16	A. N. Gibb account	£1
B	Anglia Ltd account	£32	suspense account *and*	£1
			A. N. Gibb account	£1
C	A. N. Gibb account	£16	Anglia Ltd account	£1
D	Anglia Ltd account *and*	£16	suspense account	£3
	A. N. Gibb account	£16		

19 A cheque was cashed for £10 petty cash, but this was completely omitted from the books

	Debit		Credit	
A	bank account	£10	petty cash account	£10
B	petty cash account	£10	bank account	£10
C	suspense account	£10	petty cash account	£10
D	suspense account	£10	bank account	£10

20 The payment of wages in cash £5, was entered twice in the books by mistake

	Debit		Credit	
A	wages account	£5	suspense account	£5
B	suspense account	£5	wages account	£5
C	wages account	£5	cash account	£5
D	cash account	£5	wages account	£5

When you have checked the answers to questions 7 to 20 it would be a useful exercise to assume that all the mistakes were made in the same financial year, and to calculate the balance on the suspense account before the corrections are made. You could also calculate the overall change that the corrections would make to the net profit, assuming that the final accounts had been prepared before the mistakes were found.

6. DEPRECIATION

1 If the straight line method of depreciation is used, the depreciation charge is

    A a fixed percentage of the cost of the asset each year
    B a percentage of the book value of the asset each year
    C always 10% of the cost of the asset each year
    D a fluctuating percentage of the cost of the asset each year

2 Firms charge depreciation each year

    A to ensure there is enough money in the firm to replace the asset
    B to spread the cost of the asset over its working life
    C to reduce the profit and thus reduce the dividends they can pay to shareholders
    D because the law states they must

3 Which of the following assets is most likely to appreciate rather than depreciate?

    A Plant and machinery
    B Land and buildings
    C Motor vehicles
    D Fixtures and fittings

For questions 4, 5 and 6 select your answer by means of the following code:

    A if 1, 2 and 3 are correct
    B if 1 and 2 only are correct
    C if only 1 is correct
    D if only 3 is correct

4 Depreciation is caused by

    1 obsolescence
    2 wear and tear
    3 passage of time

5 Which of the following methods can be used to calculate depreciation?

    1 Straight line
    2 Reducing balance
    3 Revaluation

6 The Companies Acts state that Companies' Final Published Accounts must show

    1 depreciation charged during the past year
    2 the balance on the provision for depreciation account
    3 the method of calculating depreciation

7 Another name for the Equal Instalment method of depreciation is the

    A reducing balance method
    B sinking fund method
    C straight line method
    D revaluation method

8 An asset is purchased for £1100. The scrap value is £100 and it is expected to last ten years. The amount of straight line depreciation charged each year would be

    A £90
    B £100
    C £110
    D £120

9 A firm does not keep its asset accounts at cost. The entries for depreciation at the end of the year should be

	Debit	*Credit*
A	asset account	bank account
B	provision for depreciation account	profit and loss account
C	asset account	profit and loss account
D	profit and loss account	asset account

10 A firm keeps its asset accounts at cost. The entries for depreciation at the end of the year should be

	Debit	*Credit*
A	profit and loss account	provision for depreciation account
B	provision for depreciation account	asset account
C	profit and loss account	bank account
D	profit and loss account	asset account

11 A firm buys an asset for £1000 and depreciates it using the diminishing balance method. Which of the following amounts would be the second year's depreciation charge at 10% per annum?

    A £80
    B £81
    C £90
    D £100

continue overleaf

12 On 1st January a firm's loose tools are valued at £450. A year later they are revalued at £300. The depreciation charge for the year is

  A £50
  B £100
  C £150
  D £300

13 The book value of a motor van on 1st January is £2000. Two years later the book value is £1000. The straight line depreciation rate of charge each year is

  A 12½%
  B 25%
  C 33⅓%
  D 50%

14 The vehicles in a company's fleet usually last three years. It would probably charge depreciation on a fixed instalment basis at a rate of

  A 25% per annum
  B 33⅓% per annum
  C 50% per annum
  D 66⅔% per annum

15 A firm buys a lathe for £2000 on 1st January and another one for £2400 on 1st July. Depreciation is charged at the rate of 10% per annum on cost, using the basis of one month's ownership needs one month's depreciation. The total depreciation charge on the 31st December should be

  A £220
  B £320
  C £360
  D £440

16 An asset costs £1200 and is expected to last ten years, so depreciation is charged at £120 per year. However, after ten years the asset is still in use. Which of the following would be the future charge for depreciation?

  A Continue to charge £120 per year depreciation
  B Credit profit and loss account with £120 every year the asset continues to be in use
  C Stop charging depreciation after the ten years
  D Reduce the depreciation charge on another asset

17 An asset has a book value of £300 but is sold for £400. The double entry should be

	Debit		*Credit*	
A	asset account	£100	profit and loss account	£100
B	cash account	£400	asset account *and*	£300
			profit and loss account	£100
C	profit and loss account	£400	cash account	£400
D	cash account	£400	profit and loss account	£400

18 The balance at cost of an asset in the ledger is £500. The balance on the provision for depreciation account of the asset is £400. If the asset is sold for £50, the double entry should be

	Debit		*Credit*	
A	bank account	£50	profit and loss account	£50
B	bank account *and*	£50	asset account	£450
	provision for depreciation account	£400		
C	profit and loss account *and*	£450	asset account	£500
	bank account	£50		
D	bank account,	£50	asset account	£500
	provision for depreciation account *and*	£400		
	profit and loss account	£50		

19 A firm's assets at cost total £10 000. The total depreciation charged to date is £4,500. The book value of the assets is

    A £4500
    B £5500
    C £10 000
    D £14 500

20 The cost of a firm's assets three years ago was £24 000. Depreciation was charged at the rate of 10% per annum by the straight line method. It decided to change its method to diminishing balance at 10% per annum, with retrospective effect. The total difference in the profits over the three years would be

    A £669
    B £696
    C £966
    D £969

7. BAD DEBTS AND PROVISIONS FOR BAD DEBTS

1 To write off a debt as bad the correct procedure is to

	Debit	Credit
A	debtor's account	bad debts account
B	debtor's account	provision for bad debts account
C	bad debts account	debtor's account
D	provision for bad debts account	profit and loss account

2 Smith owes you £100 and Jones owes you £250. Both debtors are declared bankrupt but you are to receive dividends of 25% and 40% respectively. The bad debts total

    A £125   **B** £175   **C** £200   **D** £225

3 At the end of the financial year the entries regarding bad debts are

	Debit	Credit
A	profit and loss account	bad debts account
B	bad debts account	profit and loss account
C	debtors account	provision for bad debts account
D	provision for bad debts account	profit and loss appropriation account

4 Four years ago Johnston and Co.'s account was written off as a bad debt. If a cheque is now received from them for the amount that was written off, the correct procedure is to

	Debit	Credit
A	bank account	provision for bad debts account
B	bad debts account	Johnston and Co. account
C	Johnston and Co. account	profit and loss account
D	bank account	profit and loss account

5 Firms make provisions for bad debts in order to

    A avoid having any bad debts
    B get their debtors to pay more quickly
    C keep the debtors' figure approximately the same value each year
    D obtain a 'true and fair' debtors' figure for the balance sheet

6 Provisions for bad debts should appear on the balance sheet as

    A a fictitious asset
    B part of the share capital
    C a deduction from the debtors
    D an addition to the goodwill

7 To make a provision for bad debts the correct procedure is to

	Debit	*Credit*
A	provision for bad debts account	bad debts account
B	debtors' account	provision for bad debts account
C	provision for bad debts account	profit and loss account
D	profit and loss account	provision for bad debts account

8 A firm has debtors of £5000 and a provision for bad debts of £450. The firm wishes to increase its provision to 10% of the debtors. The correct procedure would be to

	Debit		*Credit*	
A	provision for bad debts account	£50	profit and loss account	£50
B	profit and loss account	£50	provision for bad debts account	£50
C	profit and loss account	£500	provision for bad debts account	£500
D	provision for bad debts account	£500	profit and loss account	£500

9 A firm has a bad debts provision of £15 and debtors of £180. The firm wishes to make the provision equal to 5% of the debtors. It should

	Debit		*Credit*	
A	profit and loss account	£6	provision for bad debts account	£6
B	profit and loss account	£9	provision for bad debts account	£9
C	provision for bad debts account	£9	profit and loss account	£9
D	provision for bad debts account	£6	profit and loss account	£6

continue overleaf

10   On 31st December the following balances existed in a firm's books. Debtors £3000, Bad debts written off £50, Provision for bad debts £200. The firm requires a provision for bad debts to be made of 10% of the debtors. It should

	Debit		*Credit*	
A	profit and loss account	£95	provision for bad debts account	£
B	profit and loss account	£295	provision for bad debts account	£
C	profit and loss account	£300	provision for bad debts account	£
D	profit and loss account	£100	provision for bad debts account	£

Look at the following accounts and then answer questions 11 to 16. The financial year runs from 1st January to 31st December and all dates are in the same year.

Debtors Account

| 1 Jan. Balance | £5000 | | |

Bad Debts Account

	£		£
1 June Debtors	100	31 Dec. Profit and Loss	150
1 Sept. Debtors	50		
	£150		£150

Provision for Bad Debts Account

	£		£
31 Dec. Profit and Loss	50	1 Jan. Balance	250
31 Dec. Balance c/f	200		
	£250		£250
		Balance b/f	200

Extract from Profit and Loss Account for the year ended 31 December 19—

| 31 Dec. Bad Debts | £150 | 31 Dec. Provision for Bad Debts | £50 |

---

11   If the provision for bad debts account is adjusted at the end of this financial year to equal 5% of the debtors, the balance on the total debtors account at 31st December must have been

  A £1000
  B £2500
  C £4000
  D £5000

12   The 'net' figure for debtors which appeared in the balance sheet at the end of the previous year was

  A £4750
  B £4800
  C £5150
  D £5250

13   The percentage of the provision for bad debts to debtors made at the end of the previous year was

  A 4%
  B 5%
  C $7\frac{1}{2}$%
  D 10%

14   The effect on the profit for the year of all the transactions regarding debtors, bad debts and provision for bad debts is

  A a decrease of £150
  B a decrease of £100
  C an increase of £50
  D an increase of £150

15   If the £100 bad debts had NOT been written off, the overall effect on the profit for the year of all the entries relating to debtors, bad debts and provisions for bad debts would have been

  A nil
  B a decrease of £50
  C an increase of £50
  D an increase of £100

16   Which one of the following statements is INCORRECT?

From the information given in the accounts we know

  A how many debts were written off during the year as bad
  B whether the provision for bad debts was increased or decreased
  C the balance on the debtors' account at the end of the year
  D the effect the bad debts have had on the profit for the year

continue overleaf

17   Select your answer by means of the following code:

   A if 1, 2 and 3 are correct
   B if 1 and 2 only are correct
   C if only 1 is correct
   D if only 3 is correct

   Which of the following statements about bad debts is/are correct?
   1 A bad debt is an expense to a firm.
   2 A bad debt reduces the assets of a firm.
   3 A bad debt will never be paid.

18   Which one of the following statements about debtors, bad debts and provisions for bad debts is INCORRECT?
   A Debtors usually appear as a current asset in the balance sheet.
   B Provisions for bad debts usually have a debit balance in the ledger.
   C The bad debts account usually has a debit balance in the ledger.
   D An increase in the provision for bad debts account will reduce the profit of the firm.

19   Select your answer by means of the following code:

   A if 1, 2 and 3 are correct
   B if 1 and 2 only are correct
   C if only 1 is correct
   D if only 3 is correct

   Which of the following statements about debtors is/are CORRECT?

   1 Some firms do not have any debtors.
   2 A debtor who pays his account twice by mistake, may show up as a credit balance in your ledger.
   3 A cheque received from a debtor which is subsequently dishonoured will reduce the value of debtors.

20   Which one of the following types of business is likely to have the largest amount of 'book debts'?

   A A Chinese take-away
   B A newsagent
   C A bank
   D A supermarket

8. CONTROL ACCOUNTS

1 Select your answer by means of the following code:

    A if 1, 2 and 3 are correct
    B if 1 and 2 only are correct
    C if only 1 is correct
    D if only 3 is correct

Control accounts are used to

    1 locate errors in the ledger
    2 make fraud more difficult
    3 help check expenses

2 If the sales ledger control has a debit balance of £3940 it means that

    A there is £3940 in the bank account
    B customers owe you £3940
    C you owe suppliers £3940
    D you owe expenses totalling £3940

3 If the purchase ledger control has a credit balance of £4800 it means that

    A your bank account is overdrawn by £4800
    B customers owe you £4800
    C you owe suppliers £4800
    D you owe expenses totalling £4800

4 The information for the control accounts is obtained from the

    A ledger
    B books of original entry
    C bank statements
    D final accounts

5 The total credit sales for the month should be entered on the

    A debit side of the purchase control account
    B credit side of the purchase control account
    C credit side of the sales control account
    D debit side of the sales control account

continue overleaf

6 The total of the cheques paid to suppliers in a month should be entered on the

    A debit side of the purchase control account
    B credit side of the purchase control account
    C credit side of the sales control account
    D debit side of the sales control account

7 The Eastern Company has a debit balance in your sales ledger of £400 and a credit balance of £230 in your purchase ledger. If a 'set off' is arranged the entries in your control accounts should be

	Debit		*Credit*	
A	purchase control account	£400	sales control account	£400
B	purchase control account	£170	sales control account	£170
C	purchase control account	£230	sales control account	£230
D	sales control account	£170	purchase control account	£170

8 The total of the cheques received from customers in a month should be entered on the

    A debit side of the purchase control account
    B credit side of the purchase control account
    C credit side of the sales control account
    D debit side of the sales control account

9 The total of the returns outwards for the month should be entered on the

    A debit side of the purchase control account
    B credit side of the purchase control account
    C credit side of the sales control account
    D debit side of the sales control account

10 Select your answer by means of the following code:

    A if 1, 2 and 3 are correct
    B if 1 and 2 only are correct
    C if only 1 is correct
    D if only 3 is correct

Which of the following circumstances would give rise to a credit balance existing on an account in the sales ledger?

1 A customer who twice pays his account in full, by mistake
2 Returns by a customer after he has paid his account in full
3 The writing off of a bad debt

11 Additional freight costs charged to a customer should be entered on the

A debit side of the purchase control account
B credit side of the purchase control account
C credit side of the sales control account
D debit side of the sales control account

12 Cash discounts received should be entered on the

A debit side of the purchase control account
B credit side of the purchase control account
C credit side of the sales control account
D debit side of the sales control account

13 Select your answer by means of the following code:

A if 1, 2 and 3 are correct
B if 1 and 2 only are correct
C if only 1 is correct
D if only 3 is correct

Which of the following circumstances would give rise to a debit balance existing on an account in the purchase ledger?

1 An overpayment by mistake to a supplier in full settlement of his account
2 Returns to a supplier after the account had been paid in full
3 A letter from a supplier, after the account had been paid in full, stating that you had been overcharged

14 The totals of the returns inwards book for the month should be entered on the

A debit side of the purchase control account
B credit side of the purchase control account
C credit side of the sales control account
D debit side of the sales control account

15 The total purchases on credit for the month should be entered on the

A debit side of the purchase control account
B credit side of the purchase control account
C credit side of the sales control account
D debit side of the sales control account

continue overleaf

16 Select your answer by means of the following code:

    A if 1, 2 and 3 are correct
    B if 1 and 2 only are correct
    C if only 1 is correct
    D if only 3 is correct

    A reduction in the provision for bad debts is entered in the

    1 sales control account
    2 sales ledger
    3 profit and loss account

17 Cash discount allowed should be entered on the

    A debit side of the purchase control account
    B credit side of the purchase control account
    C credit side of the sales control account
    D debit side of the sales control account

18 Bad debts written off are entered on the
    A debit side of the purchase control account
    B credit side of the purchase control account
    C credit side of the sales control account
    D debit side of the sales control account

19 At the end of the financial year, once the balances on the control accounts are agreed with the total balances from their respective ledgers, they should appear in the balance sheet as

    A fictitious assets and debentures
    B debtors' and creditors' balances
    C fixed assets and long term liabilities
    D fixed assets and share capital

20 A cheque received which has now been dishonoured should be entered on the

    A debit side of the purchase control account
    B credit side of the purchase control account
    C credit side of the sales control account
    D debit side of the sales control account

9. BANK RECONCILIATION STATEMENTS AND PETTY CASH

1 A bank reconciliation statement reconciles the

    A ledger with the journals
    B petty cash book with the bank account
    C bank statement with the cash book
    D day books with the bank statement

2 Select your answer by means of the following code:

    A if 1, 2 and 3 are correct
    B if 1 and 2 only are correct
    C if only 1 is correct
    D if only 3 is correct

Which of the following would cause discrepancy between a firm's cash book and bank statement?

1 Cheques drawn have not been presented for payment.
2 Cheques paid in have not been recorded on the bank statement.
3 Bank charges have not been entered in the firm's cash book.

3 A debit balance in a firm's cash book will be shown as

    A a debit balance on the bank statement
    B a credit balance on the bank statement
    C a nil balance on the bank statement
    D an overdrawn balance on the bank statement

4 Select your answer by means of the following code:

    A if 1, 2 and 3 are correct
    B if 1 and 2 only are correct
    C if only 1 is correct
    D if only 3 is correct

Which of the following statements is/are CORRECT?

1 A bank reconciliation statement tells you the balance at the bank on a particular date.
2 A bank reconciliation statement is not part of the double entry system.
3 A bank reconciliation statement is a book of original entry.

continue overleaf

Look at the following figures and then answer questions 5, 6 and 7

NOTES	DETAIL		DEBIT	CREDIT	DATE	BALANCE
	Everymans Bank Ltd				31st July	
	Statement of Account					
	Miller Enterprises Ltd				90651230	
	Balance forward				30 JUNE	126.04 CR
		107336	14.33			
		107337	13.40			
		107334	12.92		3 JUL	85.39 CR
000472194		DDR	50.00		4 JUL	35.39 CR
	Counter Credit			56.80	6 JUL	92.19 CR
		BGC		25.00	14 JUL	117.19 CR
		107338	4.00			
		107339	24.00			
		107442	100.00		18 JUL	10.81 DR
		STO	30.00		24 JUL	40.81 DR
		107444	15.00		31 JUL	55.81 DR
	INTEREST		3.00		31 JUL	58.81 DR

BOOKS OF MILLER ENTERPRISES LTD					
Cash Book					
JUL 1st	Balance	126.04	JUL 2nd	Smith	14.33
13th	White	56.80	2nd	Jones	12.92
			15th	Black	4.00
			15th	Grey	24.00
			31st	Smith	15.00
			31st	Jones	22.00
			31st	Clark	18.00

5 According to the books of Miller Enterprises Ltd the balance at the bank on 31st July was

    A £58.81
    B £72.59
    C £126.59
    D £182.84

6 According to the bank statement the balance of Miller Enterprises Ltd on 31st July was

    A £58.81 overdrawn
    B £126.04 overdrawn
    C £58.81
    D £126.04

7 The correct balance of Miller Enterprises Ltd on 31st July is

    A £98.81 overdrawn
    B £42.01 overdrawn
    C £97.59
    D £196.40

8 Assuming that it reconciles with the cash book, a credit balance on a bank statement on the 31st December would appear in the balance sheet as a

    A current asset
    B current liability
    C fixed asset
    D long term liability

9 When the monthly bank statement is sent out which one of the following would appear?

    A Cheques written but not yet presented for payment
    B Credit transfers received from customers
    C Payments into the bank not yet credited
    D A sales ledger balance written off as a bad debt

10 Which one of the following would be entered in the cash book and not on the bank statement?

    A Bank charges
    B A dishonoured cheque
    C Payments into the bank but not yet credited
    D A credit transfer received from a customer

continue overleaf

11 When drawing up a bank reconciliation statement, if you start with a debit balance as per the bank statement, the unpresented cheques should be

    A added
    B subtracted
    C multiplied
    D divided

12 When drawing up a bank reconciliation statement, if you start with a debit balance in the cash book, the bank charges should be

    A added
    B subtracted
    C multiplied
    D divided

13 Select your answer by means of the following code:
    A if 1, 2 and 3 are correct
    B if 1 and 2 only are correct
    C if only 1 is correct
    D if only 3 is correct

Which of the following items of information required for his cash book would a proprietor obtain from his bank statement

    1 Interest charged by the bank
    2 Credit transfers received by the bank
    3 Cheques received by the proprietor

14 When the monthly bank statement is sent out which one of the following would NOT appear?

    A Interest charged by the bank
    B A dishonoured cheque
    C A direct debit
    D A payment from petty cash

15 Select your answer by means of the following code:

    A if 1, 2 and 3 are correct
    B if 1 and 2 only are correct
    C if only 1 is correct
    D if only 3 is correct
Which of the following would be used as an original document for entries in the cash book?

    1 The paying-in book counterfoils
    2 The cheque book counterfoils
    3 The bank statement

16 The petty cash is kept on the IMPREST system and the balance at the start of the month is £100. If petty cash expenses during the month of £72 are incurred, the amount received from the cashier at the start of the next month should be

    A £28
    B £72
    C £100
    D £172

17 The main purpose of petty cash is

    A to pay employees' wages
    B to pay suppliers for their goods
    C as change for the till
    D to pay small day to day business expenses

18 An analytical petty cash book

    A lists different petty cash expenses under their relevant headings
    B is used instead of a three column cash book
    C is not part of the double entry system
    D is always run on the imprest system

19 Under the IMPREST system the petty cash is

    A increased every week
    B reduced every week
    C always restored to the original amount
    D used up completely before being restored

20 Select your answer by means of the following code:

    A if 1, 2 and 3 are correct
    B if 1 and 2 only are correct
    C if only 1 is correct
    D if only 3 is correct

Which of the following would be used as an original document for petty cash entries?

    1 A bus ticket
    2 Petty cash vouchers
    3 A window cleaning bill

10. THE ACCOUNTS OF CLUBS AND SOCIETIES

1 A receipts and payments account is similar to

    A an income and expenditure account
    B a statement of affairs
    C a cash or bank account
    D a profit and loss account

2 A club's income and expenditure account performs the same function as a firm's

    A trading, profit and loss account
    B balance sheet
    C bank account
    D petty cash book

3 A club's balance sheet may be referred to as its

    A income and expenditure account
    B receipts and payments account
    C accumulated fund
    D statement of affairs

4 A club's capital may be referred to as its

    A bank balance
    B assets
    C accumulated fund
    D surplus

5 A club's loss is often referred to as

    A a balance
    B a deficit
    C a surplus
    D drawings

6 The amount of members' subscriptions paid in advance is

    A an asset
    B an expense
    C a liability
    D a surplus

7 If a club owned a bar, the amount of profit or loss made by the bar in a financial year would be shown in the

    A receipts and payments account
    B income and expenditure account
    C balance sheet
    D bank account

8 A club has 100 members and the subscription is £1 per year. All have paid the right amount except three members who paid £2 each because they owed for the previous year, and one member who also paid for next year. The income from subscriptions for the year in the income and expenditure account should be

    A £96
    B £100
    C £103
    D £104

9 £400 spent on a snooker table should be entered in the

    A receipts and payments account only
    B receipts and payments account and the income and expenditure account
    C receipts and payments account and the statement of affairs
    D income and expenditure account and the statement of affairs

10 Depreciation written off the snooker table should be entered in the

    A receipts and payments account only
    B receipts and payments account and the income and expenditure account
    C receipts and payments account and the statement of affairs
    D income and expenditure account and the statement of affairs

continue overleaf

Receipts and Payments Account for the year ended 31 December 19—

Receipts	£	Payments	£
Subscriptions	104	Rent	35
Donations	70	Rates	13
Dance receipts	45	Lighting and heating	27
Sweet shop receipts	60	Insurance	10
		Dance expenses	41
		Games equipment	11
		Purchase of sweets	42
		Balance 31 December	100
	£279		£279

Income and Expenditure Account for the year ended 31 December 19—

Expenditure	£	Income	£
Loss from the sale of sweets	3	Subscriptions	
Rent	40	(100 @ £1 per annum)	100
Rates	10	Donations	70
Light and heat	27	Surplus from dances	4
Insurance	10		
Depreciation of games equipment	2		
Surplus of income over expenditure	82		
	£174		£174

Notes

1 No stocks of sweets exist at the 31st December, but an amount is owed to creditors for supplies of sweets.
2 Four members have not yet paid their subscriptions for the year covered by the accounts, but some members have paid for the following year.
3 This is the first year of the club's existence.

11 During the year the cash figure has increased by

   A £82   **B** £100   **C** £182   **D** £279

12 The accumulated fund at the beginning of the club's second year amounted to

   A £82   **B** £100   **C** £182   **D** £279

13 Rent owing at the end of the year amounted to

   A nil   **B** £5   **C** £35   **D** £40

14 Rates owing at the end of the year amounted to

   A nil   **B** £3   **C** £10   **D** £13

15 The amount owed to creditors for supplies of sweets at 31st December was

   A £3   **B** £21   **C** £42   **D** £60

16 Assuming that the subscription is to remain at £1 for the following year, and the membership is to remain the same, how many members have paid in advance for next year?

   A 2   **B** 4   **C** 6   **D** 8

17 The book value of fixed assets at 31st December amounted to

   A £2   **B** £7   **C** £9   **D** £11

18 If the donations had been 'capitalized', the accumulated fund at 31st December would have been

   A £70   **B** £82   **C** £152   **D** £174

19 If the donations had been 'capitalized', the surplus would have been

   A £12   **B** £70   **C** £82   **D** £152

20 The current assets at 31st December amounted to

   A £100   **B** £104   **C** £107   **D** £110

11. INCOMPLETE RECORDS

1 The rate of turnover of stock is the

    A total value of turnover
    B average stock divided by the cost of sales
    C number of times the average stock is sold
    D average of the opening and closing stock

2 The cost of goods sold is the

    A average stock divided by the rate of turnover of stock
    B average stock multiplied by the turnover
    C rate of turnover of stock divided by the average stock
    D average stock multiplied by the rate of turnover of stock

3 The average stock is

    A $\dfrac{\text{opening stock } plus \text{ closing stock}}{12}$

    B $\dfrac{\text{cost of goods sold}}{\text{rate of stockturn}}$

    C $\dfrac{\text{rate of stockturn}}{\text{cost of goods sold}}$

    D $\dfrac{\text{purchases}}{\text{opening stock}}$

4 Which one of the following is most likely to have the lowest rate of stockturn?

    A A supermarket
    B A greengrocer
    C A newsagent
    D A jeweller

5 If a supermarket marks up its goods for resale by 10% on cost, the gross profit made on £100 worth of goods purchased should be

    A £10
    B £90
    C £100
    D £110

6 If the sales of a retail store during a year amount to £40 000 and the store adds 33⅓% to the cost of its sales, the gross profit is

    A £6000
    B £8000
    C £10 000
    D £12 000

7 During a year a store makes a gross profit of £8000 which is 20% of the cost of goods sold. The sales must therefore be

    A £40 000
    B £48 000
    C £52 000
    D £56 000

8 During a year a store's sales are £50 000 and expenses are 20% of the gross profit. If 25% is added to the cost price of goods to obtain the selling price, the net profit is

    A £2500
    B £5500
    C £8000
    D £10 000

9 A trader wants to calculate his net profit for the previous year but he only has the following information available for the year in question

Capital at 1st January	£10 000
Capital at 31st December	£14 000
Drawings during the year	£5000

A £3000 win on the football pools was also paid into the business bank account during the year. His net profit is

    A £4000
    B £6000
    C £9000
    D £12 000

10 Calculate a trader's drawings from the following information

Opening capital	£2000
Closing capital	£2300
Net profit	£500

His drawings are

    A £100
    B £200
    C £400
    D £500

continue overleaf

11 A trader starts a business with £1000 cash and a van worth £500. At the end of his first year he has £200 in the bank, stock worth £500, debtors valued at £200 and the van which is now worth £400. If he has withdrawn £200 from the business during the year for private expenses, he has made

    A a loss of £100
    B neither a profit nor a loss
    C a profit of £100
    D a profit of £200

12 A store's mark up is the

    A gross profit expressed as a percentage of the cost of goods sold
    B gross profit expressed as a percentage of the sales
    C net profit expressed as a percentage of the cost of goods sold
    D net profit expressed as a percentage of the sales

13 A store's margin is the

    A gross profit expressed as a percentage of the cost of goods sold
    B gross profit expressed as a percentage of the sales
    C net profit expressed as a percentage of the cost of goods sold
    D net profit expressed as a percentage of the sales

14 A trader uses his business bank account and writes cheques totalling £2500 for his private use. He also takes stock valued at £900 from the shelves for his own use, and decides to give his daughter one of the firm's typewriters valued at £120 as she is starting a secretarial course at the local college. His drawings for the year total

    A £2500
    B £2620
    C £3400
    D £3520

15 If a store's mark up is 25%, the margin must be

    A 5%
    B 10%
    C 15%
    D 20%

16 If a store's margin is 40%, the mark up must be

    A 25%
    B $33\frac{1}{3}$%
    C 50%
    D $66\frac{2}{3}$%

17 Ten people formed a partnership and contributed £10 each to the venture. The total capital was used to purchase goods which were resold at a mark up of 100% on cost. If expenses were 25% of sales and the net profit was distributed equally to the partners, each partner has increased his initial capital by

    A 25%
    B 50%
    C 75%
    D 100%

18 A firm has debtors totalling £65 and one year later this has fallen to £40. The cash book indicates that £3225 was received from credit customers during the year. Assuming that there have been no bad debts and that no discount has been allowed, the sales on credit for the year must be

    A £3200
    B £3225
    C £3240
    D £3265

19 A firm owes £20 to trade creditors at the start of the year and £30 at the end. Purchases on credit during the year totalled £1000. If suppliers allowed a total of £50 cash discount during the year, the amount paid to the creditors must have been

    A £920
    B £940
    C £960
    D £980

20 A firm's debtors fell from £100 at the start of the year to £90 at the end. The total of the sales day book was £790 and the cash book showed that £770 was received from debtors during the year. Assuming a bad debt of £10 was written off, the cash discount allowed to credit customers during the year must have amounted to

    A £20
    B £40
    C £70
    D £90

12. MANUFACTURING ACCOUNTS

1 The main purpose of a manufacturing account is to find the

    A cost of overheads
    B cost of raw materials used
    C cost of production
    D gross profit

2 Which one of the following would NOT be included in the prime cost?

    A Manufacturing wages
    B Direct power
    C Direct factory expenses
    D Heating and lighting of the factory

3 Which one of the following is NOT an overhead?

    A Cost of raw materials
    B Depreciation of plant and machinery
    C Rent and rates of the factory
    D Foreman's wages

4 An alternative expression for indirect expenses is

    A prime cost
    B production cost
    C work in progress
    D overheads

5 Select your answer by means of the following code:

    A if 1, 2 and 3 are correct
    B if 1 and 2 only are correct
    C if only 1 is correct
    D if only 3 is correct

Current assets include

    1 Stock of finished goods
    2 Stock of work in progress
    3 Stock of raw materials

6 The prime cost consists of

    A wages plus overheads
    B materials plus overheads
    C all direct factory expenses
    D indirect factory expenses

7 Work in progress at the end of the financial year is

    A included in the present year's production cost
    B not included in the present year's production cost
    C included in the previous year's production cost
    D added to the cost of raw materials

8 If the prime cost is £4000, overheads £6000, work in progress at 1st January £1000 and work in progress at 31st December £2000, the cost of the year's production of finished goods is

    A £9000
    B £10 000
    C £11 000
    D £13 000

9 Depreciation of plant and machinery is usually classified as

    A a financial cost
    B an overhead cost
    C a selling cost
    D an administration cost

10 If a manufacturing company has to pay a royalty for every unit it produces, this would probably be classified as

    A an indirect cost
    B a direct cost
    C an overhead
    D a cost of materials

11 Which one of the following is usually classified as a variable cost in the short term?

    A Cost of materials used
    B Factory rates
    C Factory rent
    D Foreman's wages

continue overleaf

12 Which one of the following is usually classified as a fixed cost in the short term?

    A Direct labour costs
    B Power for the factory machinery
    C Cost of materials used
    D Factory rent and rates

13 In a manufacturing firm's trading account the cost of production figure replaces the

    A cost of goods sold
    B closing stock of finished goods
    C purchases of finished goods
    D gross profit

Look at the following manufacturing account and then answer questions 14 to 20

Manufacturing Account for the year ended 31 December 19—

	£
Opening stock of raw materials	15 000
Purchases of raw materials	50 000
Carriage on raw materials	2 000
	67 000
Less closing stock of raw materials	7 000
	60 000
Manufacturing wages	45 000
Direct power	5 000
	110?00
Depreciation of machinery	10 000
Light and heat	6 000
Indirect wages	?
Rent and rates	12 000
Maintenance	1 000
	142 000
Add Work in progress at 1 January	?
	?
Less Work in progress at 31 December	5 000
TOTAL	£141 000

14 The cost of raw materials used is

    A £50 000   **B** £60 000   **C** £65 000   **D** £67 000

15 The prime cost is

    A £60 000   **B** £67 000   **C** £110 000   **D** £142 000

16 The total factory overheads are

    A £23 000   **B** £32 000   **C** £141 000   **D** £142 000

17 The cost of the year's production of finished goods is

    A £110 000   **B** £141 000   **C** £142 000   **D** £146 000

18 The work in progress at the start of the year was

    A £1000   **B** £3000   **C** £4000   **D** £5000

19 The indirect wages for the year totalled

    A £1000   **B** £2000   **C** £3000   **D** £4000

20 If the accountant had forgotten to take into account that £500 paid for factory rates was for the following year, the production cost would have been

    A £140 500   **B** £141 000   **C** £141 500   **D** £142 000

13. PARTNERSHIP ACCOUNTS

1 Select your answer by means of the following code:

    A if 1, 2 and 3 are correct
    B if 1 and 2 only are correct
    C if only 1 is correct
    D if only 3 is correct

When there is no written agreement partnerships are governed by the Partnership Act, 1890. Which of the following is included in this act?

    1 Loans to partners will receive an interest of 5% per annum
    2 No partners shall receive a salary
    3 Profits and losses are shared in proportion to capitals

2 At the end of the financial year a partner's drawings are transferred to the

    A credit side of the partner's capital account
    B credit side of the partner's current account
    C debit side of the partnership's bank account
    D debit side of the partner's current account

3 After the final accounts have been prepared, a debit balance on a partner's current account means that the

    A partner is owed that amount by the partnership
    B partnership's bank account is overdrawn
    C partner is in debt to the partnership for that amount
    D partnership has no working capital

4 If a partnership makes a loss during the financial year, this is

    A debited to the partners' current accounts
    B credited to the partners' current accounts
    C credited to the partnership's bank account
    D debited to the partners' salaries accounts

5 If one partner receives a salary which is credited to him at the end of the year, the share of the profit available for distribution will be

    A increased
    B decreased
    C unchanged
    D non-existent

6 The entries for the appropriation of profit should be

	Debit	*Credit*
A	partners' capital accounts	partners' current accounts
B	partnership bank account	partners' current accounts
C	profit and loss appropriation account	partners' current accounts
D	partners' current accounts	profit and loss appropriation account

7 If a partner withdraws some stock for his own use, the entries should be

	Debit	*Credit*
A	partner's current account	purchases account
B	purchases account	partner's current account
C	stock account	profit and loss account
D	profit and loss account	stock account

8 A credit balance on a partner's current account is

    A a fixed asset
    B part of the capital
    C a long term liability
    D a current asset

9 When partners receive interest on their capital the entries should be

	Debit	*Credit*
A	current account	capital account
B	profit and loss appropriation account	current account
C	current account	profit and loss appropriation account
D	capital account	current account

10 X and Y have shared out a profit of £1,200 in equal proportions but then realize that Y should only have received 40%; the correcting entries should be

	Debit		*Credit*	
A	Y's current account	£200	X's capital account	£200
B	X's profit and loss appropriation account	£200	Y's current account	£200
C	X's current account	£120	Y's profit and loss appropriation account	£120
D	Y's capital account	£120	X's current account	£120

continue overleaf

Peters and Lever Partnership

Balance Sheet as at 31 December 19—

	Peters	Lever	Total	Fixed Assets	Cost	Provision for Depreciation	N
	£	£	£		£	£	£
Capital Accounts	10 000	8000	18 000	Land and buildings	10 000	–	10 00
Current Accounts				Machinery	5 000	500	4 50
Balance at 1 Jan.	200	100		Vehicles	4 000	2000	2 00
Interest on					19 000	2500	16 50
Capital	1000	800					
Salary	–	500		Current Assets			
Share of remaining				Stock		3500	
profit	3250	2600		Debtors	3 000		
	4450	4000		*Less* Provision			
Less Drawings	2000	1000		for bad debts	300		
Interest on						2700	
drawings	100	50		Prepayments		2500	
Balance at 31 Dec.	2350	2950	5 300	Bank		2000	
							10 70
Current Liabilities		£					
Creditors		2900					
Accruals		1000	3 900				
			£27 200				£27 20

Profits and losses are shared in proportion to capitals

---

11 The net profit of the partnership for the year was

    A £5300   **B** £5850   **C** £8000   **D** £8450

12 If the partnership was sold at its book value, Lever's share of the sale should be

    A £10 950   **B** £12 000   **C** £12 350   **D** £13 600

13 Peters and Lever receive interest on their capitals at the rate of

    A 5% p.a.   **B** 10% p.a.   **C** 15% p.a.   **D** 20% p.a.

14 Assuming the partners' drawings occurred on 1st January, the partners are charged interest on their drawings at the rate of

    A 5% p.a.   **B** 10% p.a.   **C** 15% p.a.   **D** 20% p.a.

15 If the partnership had just completed its first year of trading and had decided that the bad debts provision should be 13% of the debtors and not 10%, Peters' share of the remaining profits would have been

    A £2300   **B** £3160   **C** £3200   **D** £3340

16 If the partners shared remaining profits equally, Lever's profit share would have been

    A £2650   **B** £2925   **C** £4000   **D** £4225

17 If no interest was allowed on the partners' capital accounts, Peters' share of the profit would have been

    A £3400   **B** £4250   **C** £4300   **D** £4520

18 The total income of the partnership available for appropriation was

    A £5300   **B** £8000   **C** £8150   **D** £8450

19 If the partnership had just completed its first year of trading, had suffered a bad debt of £500 which had not yet been written off, and had kept the same percentage of provision for bad debts to debtors, Lever's share of remaining profit would have been

    A £2300   **B** £2400   **C** £3400   **D** £4500

20 If Peters decided to withdraw a motor vehicle valued at £1000 from the partnership for his own private use, the entries should be

	Debit	*Credit*
A	motor vehicles account	Peters' capital account
B	Peters' current account	motor vehicles account
C	Peters' current account	bank account
D	Peters' capital account	Peters' current account

14. FINAL ACCOUNTS OF COMPANIES

1 Joint Stock Companies are owned by the

    A debenture holders
    B shareholders
    C board of directors
    D employees

2 A company's authorized capital is the

    A amount of shares it has issued
    B amount of shares it is allowed to issue
    C total amount of capital the company is allowed to raise
    D total amount of issued capital plus reserves

3 In a company's balance sheet the item 'general reserve' appears under the heading of

    A issued capital
    B reserves required by law
    C reserves recommended by the directors
    D long term loans

4 In a company's balance sheet the item 'debentures' normally appears under the heading of

    A authorized capital
    B issued share capital
    C long term loans
    D current liabilities

5 Which one of the following should NOT appear in a company's profit and loss appropriation account?

    A Transfer to general reserve
    B Writing off goodwill
    C Payment of dividends
    D Writing off depreciation

6 Company balance sheets must show

    A assets at cost *less* total depreciation to date
    B assets at cost *less* depreciation charged that year
    C only the book value of the assets
    D only the total depreciation charged

7 Companies pay dividends as a percentage of the

    A authorized capital
    B issued capital
    C reserves
    D debentures

8 The issued capital of a company is as follows:
10 000 Ordinary shares of £1 and 5000 5% Preference shares of 50p each.

If the directors decide to recommend an ordinary dividend of 10%, the total dividends paid that year would amount to

    A £1000
    B £1125
    C £1250
    D £1375

9 Which one of the following is a company NOT allowed to use to provide funds for the payment of dividends?

    A Revenue reserves
    B General reserves
    C Capital reserves
    D Retained earnings

For questions 10 and 11 select your answer by means of the following code:
    A if 1, 2 and 3 are correct
    B if 1 and 2 only are correct
    C if only 1 is correct
    D if only 3 is correct

10 Which of the following could appear as a fictitious asset on a company's balance sheet?

    1 Preliminary expenses
    2 Provision for bad debts
    3 Motor vehicles

11 Proposed dividends
    1 reduce the reserves of the company
    2 will eventually affect the cash position
    3 appear under the heading of Current Assets in the balance sheet
continue overleaf

Look at the information on these two pages and then answer questions 12 to 20

THE BRAINTREE COMPANY LIMITED

Profit and Loss Appropriation Account for the year ended 31 December 19—

	£	£
Net trading profit (before tax)		12 000
Corporation tax		6 240
Net profit after tax		5 760
Add Retained earnings 1 January 19—		4 240
Profit available for distribution		10 000
Less appropriations:		
Preference shareholders dividend	2000	
Ordinary shareholders dividend	4000	
General reserve	1000	
Goodwill written off	500	7 500
Retained earnings 31 December 19—		£2 500

12 If you owned some preference shares in the company what would be the rate of return on your investment?

    A 5%   **B** 7½%   **C** 10%   **D** 12½%

13 If the company was sold at its book value the amount due to the ordinary shareholder would be

    A £20 000   **B** £29 500   **C** £37 500   **D** £45 740

14 The total long term capital employed is

    A £40 000   **B** £48 000   **C** £57 500   **D** £65 740

15 The ordinary shareholders have received a dividend of

    A 5%   **B** 10%   **C** 15%   **D** 20%

16 The maximum dividend that the directors could have paid the ordinary shareholders was

    A 20%   **B** 40%   **C** 60%   **D** 80%

17 The return on all long term capital employed before deducting corporation tax is approximately

    A 5%   **B** 10%   **C** 15%   **D** 20%

18 The net assets of the company are valued at

    A £46 500   **B** £50 500   **C** £57 500   **D** £65 740

THE BRAINTREE COMPANY LIMITED

Balance Sheet as at 31 December 19—

Share Capital (authorized and issued)	£	£
40 000 Preferences shares of 50p each	20 000	
20 000 Ordinary shares of £1 each	20 000	40 000
Reserves required by law		
Share premium account		2 000
Reserves recommended by the Directors		
General Reserve	5 000	
Retained Earnings	2 500	7 500
Long Term Loans		
Debentures (10%)		8 000
Current Liabilities		
Creditors	1 000	
Corporation tax	6 240	
Accruals	1 000	8 240
		£65 740

Represented by: Fixed Assets	Cost	Provision for Depreciation	Net
		£	£
Land and buildings	35 000	—	35 000
Plant and machinery	10 000	2 500	7 500
Motor vehicles	8 000	4 000	4 000
	53 000	6 500	46 500
Goodwill			4 000
Current Assets			
Stock		3 000	
Debtors (less Provision for bad debts)		6 000	
Prepayments		2 000	
Bank		4 240	15 240
			£65 740

19 On 1st January the intangible assets were valued at

    A £3000   **B** £3500   **C** £4000   **D** £4500

20 The dividends

    A have only been proposed
    B have already been paid
    C never affect the cash position of the company
    D cannot be paid because there is not enough money in the bank

15. GOODWILL AND THE PURCHASE OF A BUSINESS

For questions 1 to 6 select your answer by means of the following code:

    A if 1, 2 and 3 are correct
    B if 1 and 2 only are correct
    C if only 1 is correct
    D if only 3 is correct

1 The vendor is the person who is

    1 selling the business
    2 buying the business
    3 arranging the transfer of the business

2 Businesses may be joined together through

    1 an amalgamation
    2 a take-over bid
    3 a purchase of one business by another

3 The excess paid for a business above the net value of the assets taken over is known as

    1 a capital reserve
    2 the capital
    3 goodwill

4 If the purchaser of a business paid less than the net value of the assets taken over, this would probably be treated as

    1 a capital reserve
    2 the capital
    3 goodwill

5 Purchasers of businesses are often prepared to pay in excess of the value of the net assets because of the

    1 location of the business
    2 expertise of the labour force
    3 possession of patents and trade marks

6 Goodwill appearing in the balance sheet of a sole trader means that the sole trader

    1 must have sold his business
    2 has made a large loss that year
    3 must have purchased another business at some time

7 Goodwill is

    A a current asset
    B a wasting asset
    C an intangible asset
    D a fictitious asset

8 A company writing off goodwill should debit the

    A trading account
    B balance sheet
    C profit and loss account
    D profit and loss appropriation account

9 Goodwill is usually valued in the balance sheet of a sole trader at

    A the previous year's sales figure
    B the total assets *less* the current liabilities
    C its purchase price *less* amounts written off
    D the current assets *less* the current liabilities

10 The entries for the agreed purchase price of a business in the buyer's books are

	Debit	*Credit*
A	bank account	business purchase account
B	business purchase account	bank account
C	vendor's account	business purchase account
D	business purchase account	vendor's account

11 The total value of the assets taken over in the buyer's books is credited to the

    A vendor's account
    B capital account
    C business purchase account
    D goodwill account

12 The value of the creditors taken over when purchasing another business are credited to

    A the vendor's account
    B the business purchase account
    C the goodwill account
    D personal accounts in the bought ledger

continue overleaf

Look at the following information and then answer questions 13 to 18

Good's Balance Sheet as at 31 December 19—

Liabilities	£	Assets	£	£
Capital	8000	Premises		4000
		Plant and machinery		2000
		Furniture and fittings		1500
		Debtors	1000	
		less Provision for		
Creditors	750	bad debts	50	950
Bank overdraft	500	Stock		800
	£9250			£9250

On the basis of the above balance sheet A. Kershaw agrees to purchase all the assets and to take over the creditors. The agreed purchase price was £10 000. Kershaw then decides on the following revaluations. Plant and machinery £1800; furniture and fittings £1400; stock £750; provision for bad debts £100.
Kershaw has £7000 saved and borrows £3000 from the bank on a long term loan. He pays Good immediately.

13 The goodwill figure in Kershaw's opening balance sheet is

    A £900
    B £1400
    C £1900
    D £2100

14 The capital figure in Kershaw's opening balance sheet is

    A £7000
    B £8000
    C £9000
    D £10 000

15 The total value of the fixed assets (excluding goodwill) in Kershaw's opening balance sheet is

    A £7200
    B £7500
    C £9250
    D £10 750

16 The total value of the current assets in Kershaw's opening balance sheet is

A £1650
B £1750
C £3050
D £3450

17 The working capital in Kershaw's opening balance sheet is

A £500
B £900
C £1400
D £1900

18 The value of the current liabilities in Kershaw's opening balance sheet is

A £250
B £750
C £1250
D £3750

19 When the purchase price of a business is paid the entries in the buyer's books are

	Debit	*Credit*
A	cash book	vendor's account
B	business purchase account	cash book
C	vendor's account	cash book
D	capital account	cash book

20 Which one of the following assets is usually NOT taken over by the purchasing firm?

A Fixtures and fittings
B Bank
C Stock
D Debtors

16. INTERPRETATION OF ACCOUNTING STATEMENTS

For questions 1 and 2 select your answer by means of the following code:

   A if 1, 2 and 3 are correct
   B if 1 and 2 only are correct
   C if only 1 is correct
   D if only 3 is correct

1 Which of the following groups of people should be interested in a report of the accounts of British Petroleum Ltd?

   1 The directors of B.P. Ltd
   2 The shareholders of B.P. Ltd
   3 The employees of B.P. Ltd

2 Which of the following groups of ratios are used in appraising the financial progress of a company?

   1 Ratios appraising liquidity
   2 Ratios appraising use of assets
   3 Ratios appraising profitability

Questions 3 and 4 relate to the following:

   A $\dfrac{\text{net credit purchases}}{\text{average trade creditors}}$

   B $\dfrac{\text{net credit sales}}{\text{average trade creditors}}$

   C $\dfrac{\text{net credit purchases}}{\text{average trade debtors}}$

   D $\dfrac{\text{net credit sales}}{\text{average trade debtors}}$

3 The efficiency of the debt collection service of a company can be measured by

   A   **B**   **C**   **D**

4 Which ratio is used to calculate the length of credit allowed by suppliers?

   A   **B**   **C**   **D**

5 The current ratio measures

   A liquidity
   B investments
   C use of assets
   D profitability

6 The rate of stock turnover in a trading period is the

    A working capital *less* stock
    B value of the stock at the end of the year
    C average stock held throughout the year
    D number of times the average stock is sold

7 Which one of the following is most likely to have the highest rate of stockturn?

    A A jeweller
    B A furniture store
    C A greengrocer
    D A furrier

8 A firm is said to be overtrading when there

    A is a shortage of fixed assets
    B are many fixed assets
    C is too much working capital
    D is a shortage of working capital

9 Net profit divided by sales and expressed as a percentage measures

    A liquidity
    B investments
    C use of assets
    D profitability

10 The rate of stockturn in a trading period is usually expressed

    A in £'s
    B as a percentage
    C as a number
    D as a ratio

11 Select your answer by means of the following code:

    A if 1, 2 and 3 are correct
    B if 1 and 2 only are correct
    C if only 1 is correct
    D if only 3 is correct

Which of the statements set out below would cause a DECREASE in the following ratio assuming the number of items purchased and sold remains constant?

$$\frac{\text{Gross profit}}{\text{Sales}} \times 100 = ? \%$$

1 Cost price has been increased but selling price has not
2 There has been a greater amount of pilfering this year
3 Cost price has decreased and selling price has increased

continue overleaf

Look at the following accounts and then answer questions 12 to 20

INCOME STATEMENTS	X	Y	Z
	£	£	£
Stock at 1 Jan.	10 000	20 000	30 000
Purchases	160 000	180 000	190 000
	170 000	200 000	220 000
Stock at 31 Dec.	20 000	20 000	20 000
Cost of sales	150 000	180 000	200 000
Sales	280 000	300 000	280 000
Gross Profit	130 000	120 000	80 000
Overhead expenses	60 000	60 000	40 000
Net Profit	£ 70 000	£ 60 000	£ 40 000

BALANCE SHEETS	X	Y	Z
	£	£	£
Fixed Assets	120 000	200 000	70 000
Current Assets:			
Stock	20 000	20 000	20 000
Debtors	25 000	14 000	10 000
Bank	15 000	36 000	10 000
	£180 000	£270 000	£110 000
Capital Employed	140 000	250 000	100 000
Creditors	40 000	20 000	10 000
	£180 000	£270 000	£110 000

Questions 12 to 20 relate to the following:

    A Firm X
    B Firm Y
    C Firm Z
    D All the same

12 Which firm has the highest average stock?

    A   B   C   D

13 Which firm has the quickest stockturn?

    A   B   C   D

14 Which firm has the quickest debt collection?

    A   **B**   **C**   **D**

15 Which firm obtained the longest period of credit from their suppliers?

    A   **B**   **C**   **D**

16 Which firm has the highest current ratio?

    A   **B**   **C**   **D**

17 Which was the most profitable firm in terms of sales?

    A   **B**   **C**   **D**

18 Which firm had the better return on capital employed?

    A   **B**   **C**   **D**

19 Which firm had the highest mark up on cost?

    A   **B**   **C**   **D**

20 Which firm was the most efficient in its expenditure on overheads when compared to sales?

    A   **B**   **C**   **D**

17. REVISION TEST (*one hour*)

1 After the draft final accounts have been prepared a small quantity of stock valued at £350 is found in an old shed. The effect will be

  A an increase of £350 on the profit
  B a decrease of £350 on the profit
  C an increase of £350 in the bank account
  D a decrease of £350 in the purchases account

For questions 2 to 5 select your answer by means of the following code:

  A if 1, 2 and 3 are correct
  B if 1 and 2 only are correct
  C if only 1 is correct
  D if only 3 is correct

2 Which of the following is capital expenditure?

  1 The cost of a soft drinks machine for the works canteen
  2 The cost of a stock of drinks for the machine
  3 The cost of the electricity to operate the machine

3 Which of the following can a company normally use to raise funds at a fixed rate of dividend or interest?

  1 Preference shares
  2 Debentures
  3 Ordinary shares

4 Which of the following would cause a change in the capital of a sole trader?

  1 Payment to a creditor for goods previously supplied
  2 Purchase of a typewriter on credit for the office
  3 Depreciation of a motor vehicle

5 Which of the following transactions would affect the cash position of a sole trader?

  1 Payment to a window cleaner from petty cash
  2 Withdrawal of some money for private purposes
  3 Depreciation of a shop fitting

6 X and Y are in partnership with respective capitals of £9000 and £6000. Y has also lent the partnership £4000 for the past year. No partnership agreement has ever been drawn up. If the net profit for the year was £20 000 before charging loan interest, Y's share of remaining profits should be

    A £7920
    B £8000
    C £9900
    D £10 000

7 M. Bickers, a sole trader, made a gross profit of 20% on sales of £62 400. The cost of goods sold was

    A £12 480
    B £15 600
    C £46 800
    D £49 920

8 The subscriptions account of a club shows the following information for one financial year. Subscriptions received during the year £200; subscriptions owing at the start of the year £10; subscriptions paid in advance at the start of the year £5; subscriptions owing at the end of the year £15. There were no subscriptions in advance for next year at the end of this current financial year. If the subscription is 50p per year, the number of members at the end of the year was

    A 380
    B 400
    C 410
    D 420

9 On 1st July Clark borrowed £2000 at a rate of 10% per annum from the Business Finance Co. Ltd. Repayments are at the rate of £500 every six months plus the six-monthly interest instalment. Interest is calculated on the outstanding balance at the time the payment is due. If all the payments are made on time, the balance owing one year after the loan was obtained would be

    A £750
    B £1000
    C £1250
    D £1500

continue overleaf

10 If no distinction is made between capital and revenue expenditure the

    A figure for debtors and creditors will be incorrect
    B cash or bank figures will be incorrect
    C net profit will be incorrect
    D balance sheet will not balance

11 An alternative expression for working capital is

    A assets *less* current liabilities
    B total assets
    C net current assets
    D net assets

12 J. Huggett purchased fifty crates of goods at £100 per crate on credit from National Supplies Ltd. A deposit of £10 per crate is also charged; a similar allowance being made when the crates are returned.
A month later Huggett returned three crates of goods which were unsatisfactory, and twenty empty crates. He also sent a cheque for £3000 as part payment. The balance on National Supplies Ltd account in Huggett's ledger after the above transactions would be

    A £1430
    B £1970
    C £2000
    D £2300

13 In what way should a small loss of stock due to deterioration be recorded?

    A It is written off in the profit and loss account
    B It is mentioned as a note to the balance sheet
    C It is included in the drawings account
    D It is not usually shown as the closing stock is automatically reduced

14 An asset is purchased for £5000 on 1st January, the beginning of the financial year. Depreciation is charged at the rate of 10% per annum on cost and is calculated on the length of time the asset is in the firm's possession. If the asset is sold after 18 months for £4750, the net effect on the profit in the year of the sale is

    A a decrease of £250
    B an increase of £250
    C a decrease of £500
    D an increase of £500

15 A business may make a loss in a year yet have more money in the bank. A reason for this could be that

    A some assets were sold
    B drawings were higher this year
    C debtors were given a longer period of credit
    D there were more prepayments at the end of the year

16 Which one of the following has a credit balance in the ledger?

    A Carriage inwards
    B Carriage outwards
    C Returns inwards
    D Returns outwards

17 A company has an issued capital of 100 000 £1 (10%) preference shares and 500 000 25p ordinary shares. It has also issued £50 000 of debentures at 5%. At the end of the financial year the directors decide to recommend an ordinary dividend of 20%. The total dividends that the company will pay for that year amount to

    A £10 000
    B £25 000
    C £35 000
    D £50 000

18 The factory cost of production of finished units consists of prime cost

    A *less* factory overheads *plus* opening work in progress
        less closing work in progress
    A *plus* factory overheads *less* opening work in progress
        plus closing work in progress
    C *plus* factory overheads *plus* opening work in progress
        less closing work in progress
    D *less* factory overheads *less* opening work in progress
        plus closing work in progress

19 Which one of the following should be included in a calculation of working capital?

    A Plant and machinery
    B Goodwill
    C Work in progress
    D Debentures

continue overleaf

Look at the following document and then answer questions 20 to 25

			No. 00241

Furniture Supplies Ltd
Southend-on-Sea
Essex

To: Hughes & Co (Retail Furnishers Ltd)
High Street
Acton.   24 November 19—

QTY	DESCRIPTION		UNIT PRICE	TOTAL
4	Tables	XB4	£20	£80.00
12	Chairs	CB2	£5	£60.00
2	Desks	XX1	£45	£90.00
1	Cabinet	TT1	£20	£20.00
				£250.00
			less 20%	50.00
			TOTAL	£200.00

Terms: 2½% one month
Delivery: By road

20 The document is

A an invoice
B a statement
C a receipt
D a credit note

21 In the books of Hughes and Co., the £50 discount will

A be entered in the purchases account
B be entered in the discount received account
C be entered in the cash account
D not be entered in the accounts

22 Which of the following amounts would Hughes and Co. enter in their purchases account?

A £195
B £200
C £243.75
D £250

23   The effect on the profit of Furniture Supplies Ltd if Hughes and Co. pay the amount within a month would be a decrease of

    A £2.50
    B £5.00
    C £6.25
    D £7.50

24   Furniture Supplies Ltd would first record the transaction in their

    A purchase returns day book
    B purchase day book
    C sales day book
    D sales returns day book

25   Hughes and Co. would record the transaction in their

    A sales ledger
    B bought ledger
    C sales returns day book
    D purchase returns day book

26   The following information relates to a factory for a complete financial year. Prime cost £100 000; overheads £300 000; opening work-in-progress £30 000; closing work-in-progress £10 000. If the factory produced 20 000 completed items in the year, the unit production cost was

    A £20
    B £20.50
    C £21
    D £21.50

27   The correct heading for a statement which shows the financial position of a business at any given time is

    A trading account for the year ended—
    B profit and loss account as at —
    C trial balance for the year ended —
    D balance sheet as at —

28   If the owner of a business withdraws some cash for private expenses from the cash sales till, the adjusting entries should be

	Debit	*Credit*
A	sales account	drawings account
B	drawings account	sales account
C	bank account	drawings account
D	drawings account	bank account

continue overleaf

29 If a fire destroyed a firm's computer, and the insurance company has agreed to pay (but not yet paid), the entries should be

	Debit	*Credit*
A	bank account	fixed asset account
B	insurance company account	fixed asset account
C	bank account	insurance company account
D	profit and loss account	insurance company account

30 As an accountant, which of the following courses of action would you advise a client to take, assuming that he had been left a legacy of £10 000. The client is leaving the country in one year's time so he is only concerned with the total income he can receive over the next year. (Ignore taxation.)

A Leave his present job and start a business for £10 000 which would bring him a return of 20%. Goodwill on the sale of the business at the end of the year would amount to £1000

B Invest all the money in a bank at an annual rate of 10%. He would keep his present job at a net salary of £1500 per annum

C Purchase a house for £10 000 which would appreciate in value at the rate of 5% on the cost per year. This could be let at an annual rental of £1000. Repairs would be £300 per year. He would keep his job at £1500 net per annum

D Purchase some 8% debentures at par for £10 000, repayable in one year's time at £1.02 each. He would keep his present job at £1500 net per annum